CONTENTS

Stories by Maureen Spurgeon

First published 1998
by Brown Watson, England

Reprinted 2001, 2003, 2005, 2007,
2010, 2011, 2013, 2015, 2016, 2017,
2018 (twice), 2019

ISBN: 978-0-7097-1255-8
© 1998 Brown Watson, England
Printed in Malaysia

Christmas
Stories

Book 1

Brown Watson

ENGLAND

CHRISTMAS
ON THE
FARM

Illustrated by Stephen Holmes

It was a cold, wintry afternoon at Happydale Farm.

"Soon be Christmas!" said Farmer Merry. "Time to put a Christmas tree in the hall!"

"Soon be Christmas!" said his wife. "Time to cut the holly and mistletoe. I want some nice big bunches for the dining room."

"Soon be Christmas!" cried Jenny. "Time to make cotton wool snowballs to stick on the windows."
"And make lots of paper snow-flakes!" added Peter.

"Moo!" went Buttercup the cow.
"Who wants cotton wool snow
and paper snowflakes? You get
REAL snow outside, where we
are, not inside, in a house!"

"But there are LOTS of things inside!" said Lenny and Lucky, the two lambs. "Just see!"

"Maybe that's because most of Christmas happens indoors," said Denny the Donkey.

The animals talked about it for a long time. How they wished they could go indoors, just for once! "People talk about stars at Christmas," said Denny. "They're up in the sky! Look!"

As well as the stars, they saw something else.

"It's like the sledge that Jenny and Peter play with in the snow," said Denny. "A sleigh," said Hector the Horse.

"And those are reindeer!" added Denny. "It-it's Father Christmas, the man who brings presents on Christmas Eve!"
"Couldn't we ask him to bring us something?" cried Lucky.

"We don't want presents," said Hector. "We only want to go indoors to see what Christmas is like."

"Then that's what we'll wish for!" said Denny.

"What a good idea!" said the others.

But all that happened next morning was that Mrs. Merry put a sack of straw into her car. "Come along, Jenny and Peter!" she called. "Time for school!" It seemed very odd to the animals!

The straw was for the Nativity Play which told the story of the first Christmas, when Baby Jesus was born in a stable. Jenny was going to be Mary, the mother of Jesus.

Peter and his friends, Billy and Mark, were going to be the shepherds. "Baby Jesus needs a manger to lie in," said Miss Lane, their teacher. "What could we use for that?"

"We've got a REAL manger at our farm!" Peter said proudly.

"Dad would lend it to us, wouldn't he, Mum?"

"We could bring Lenny and Lucky to school, as well," said Jenny.

But the animals were disappointed
when they heard the news.
"We ALL wanted to see Christmas
indoors!" said Lucky.
"It's not fair, just me and Lenny
getting our wish."

"Tell us all about it when you get back!" said Hector.
"Don't forget anything!" squawked Hetty the Hen.
"I can LOOK indoors," said Denny, "and see for myself!"

Denny could see that Lucky and Lenny did not like being indoors. The children were kind and the play was lovely, but they felt hot and uncomfortable, and they missed their friends.

But Miss Lane was very pleased. "You have all worked hard!" she told the children as they got ready to go home. "Look, it's beginning to snow! Just in time for Christmas, too!"

It snowed all through the night. By next morning, the snow had stopped, but it was still very, very cold. All the pipes at school had frozen. Miss West said everyone had to go home.

"No Nativity Play today!" she said. "I am sorry, children."
"Oh, dear!" said Farmer Merry. "We've brought the manger and the lambs, too." But Denny the Donkey had an idea!

He ran down the lane, braying loudly. "Hee-haw! Hee-haw!" "He wants us to go back to Happydale Farm!" said Farmer Merry. "Everyone in the school mini-bus, Miss Lane!"

Buttercup the Cow, Hector the Horse and Hetty the Hen were surprised to see Denny leading the mini-bus towards the big barn at Happydale Farm. Everyone looked so excited!

"The perfect place for our Nativity Play!" cried Miss Lane. "Change into your costumes, children!" Soon, lots of people were crowding into the barn, waiting for the play to begin.

And as well as the lambs Lenny and Lucky, Denny the Donkey, Buttercup the Cow, Hetty the Hen and Hector the Horse all appeared together in the Nativity Play.

"So THIS is what Christmas is really about!" said Denny. "I'm glad we could share in it all."

"Well," said Hector the Horse, "that is what we wished for. Don't you remember?"

Not long afterwards, it was Christmas Eve. And as the reindeer pulled his magic sleigh across the sky, Father Christmas smiled down at all the animals on Happydale Farm.

He had brought bells for Lucky,
Lenny and Buttercup, a basket of
straw for Hetty, apples for Denny
and a blanket for Hector. How
surprised they would be on
Christmas morning!

CHRISTMAS
SONGS, CAROLS AND VERSES

Illustrated by Peter Wilks

JINGLE BELLS

Dashing through the snow
In a one horse open sleigh,
O'er the fields we go,
Laughing all the way;
Bells on bob-tail ring,
Making spirits bright,

What fun it is to ride and sing
A sleighing song tonight!
Jingle bells! Jingle bells!
Jingle all the way!
Oh, what fun it is to ride
In a one horse open sleigh!

SILENT NIGHT! HOLY NIGHT!

Silent night! Holy night!
All is calm, all is bright;
Round yon Virgin Mother and Child,
Holy Infant so tender and mild:
Sleep in heavenly peace,
Sleep in heavenly peace.

MY SNOWMAN FRIEND

I call him Mr. Frosty-Face!
He brings us so much fun,
He has coal eyes, a carrot nose
And a smile for everyone!

When I talk, I know he'll listen
To every word I say,
I can shout, or knock his hat off,
And he'll never run away!

But when the weather's warmer,
Then Frosty-Face must go –
Until the next time that he comes
With winter's ice and snow.

GOOD KING WENCESLAS

Good King Wenceslas looked out,
On the feast of Stephen,
When the snow lay round about,
Deep, and crisp, and even:

Brightly shone the moon that night,
Though the frost was cruel,
When a poor man came in sight,
Gath'ring winter fuel.

POOR OLD SANTA

We've put up the decorations
With plenty of holly to see,
We've helped Mummy to make
Mince pies and a cake,
We've got the star for our tree!

We've hung our Christmas stockings,
But the chimney we did not clean!
Now, there's soot, dirt and mess,
Santa's stuck there unless . . .
He can wait 'til the chimney
sweep's been!

AWAY IN A MANGER
Away in a manger,
No crib for a bed,
The little Lord Jesus
Laid down His sweet head;

The stars in the bright sky
Look down where He lay,
The little Lord Jesus
Asleep on the hay.

SANTA'S SLEIGH

Have you ever wondered
Where Santa leaves his sleigh,
When he brings toys for children
To find on Christmas Day?

For reindeers, all the roof-tops
Are much too smooth and steep!
One slip, they'd go sliding down,
And land in one big heap!

But if they were in the garden,
How could Santa with his sack,
Climb right up to the roof-top,
Then down the chimney stack?

There's so much danger in the road,
So, where CAN he leave his sleigh?
Perhaps you'd like to ask him,
When he comes round your way!

51

WE WISH YOU
A MERRY CHRISTMAS

We wish you a Merry Christmas,
We wish you a Merry Christmas,
We wish you a Merry Christmas
And a Happy New Year!

O CHRISTMAS TREE!

O Christmas Tree! O Christmas Tree!
Thy leaves are so unchanging:
Not only green when summer's here
But also when 'tis cold and drear.
O Christmas Tree! O Christmas Tree!
Thy leaves are so unchanging.

THE CHRISTMAS FAIRY

I am the Christmas fairy –
And everything I see,
With wand and crown,
As I look down
From the top branch of the tree!

I see the pretty coloured lights,
The cards hung on the wall,
Candies and sweets,
And Christmas-time treats
For visitors when they call.

What fun on Christmas morning!
I'll remember all I saw,
When I'm put away
Until the day
I'm on the tree, once more.

O LITTLE TOWN OF BETHLEHEM

O little town of Bethlehem,
How still we see thee lie;
Above thy deep and dreamless sleep
The silent stars go by.

Yet in thy dark streets shineth
The everlasting Light;
The hopes and fears of all the years
Are met in thee tonight.

GUESS WHO!

F is for the Fur trim
   round his big boots and hat,

A is for his Apple cheeks,
   so cuddly, round and fat!

T is for the Toys he brings, and

H his Happy smile!

E is for his Eyes, so bright, and –

R each Reindeer mile!

C is for the Chimney stack, and
H the Hearth below.
R for his Red cloak and hood,
I the Ice and snow!
S is for the Stockings,
T is for the Tree – and
M is for the Mistletoe,
   which we all love to see!
A is for the Angels,
   who on Christmas cards appear
S for dear old Santa Claus,
   who visits us each year!

CHRISTMAS IS COMING

Christmas is coming,
The goose is getting fat,
Please put a penny
In the old man's hat.
If you haven't got a penny,
A ha'penny will do;
If you haven't got a ha'penny,
Then God bless you!

SANTA'S
LITTLE HELPER

Illustrated by Colin Petty

It was always cold where Peter lived – almost as cold as the land where Santa Claus came from. And with all the ice and snow and the green fir trees reaching up to the sky, everywhere always looked Christmassy, too – especially when Peter and his dad came back from town on the sledge!

The sledge was always loaded up when Christmas was coming. Not with toys and presents, but with food, clothes and everything else Peter's family needed. A team of dogs pulled it across the snow.

Peter loved all the dogs and helped to look after each one. His favourite was Marcus, the leader. "Daddy," Peter said one day, "why does Santa Claus have reindeer to pull his sleigh?"

"I suppose because he's always had reindeer," smiled Daddy. "I just happen to like dogs best." "So do I!" said Peter. "Marcus could pull the sleigh across the sky without any trouble."

Peter went indoors to write his Christmas letter. What he wanted more than anything else was a guitar. "My Daddy could teach me how to play it," he wrote, "and everyone would enjoy the music."

Peter finished by writing about his clever dog, Marcus. But he was wondering if Father Christmas really could bring the guitar he wanted so badly. He had only ever seen a picture of one, in a book.

An icy blast of wind lifted Peter's letter up and up into the dark, wintry sky, until it was like a big snowflake, whirling round and round. Then, at last, it floated down on a cloud.

At least, it looked like a cloud to anyone who might have been watching. But really, it was a heap of letters. "We'll never get all these sorted out!" someone cried. "It's Christmas Eve, soon!"

"We'll manage!" came a jolly-sounding voice – and a big chubby hand in a red sleeve picked up Peter's letter. "How many times have I said that Christmas comes but once a year?"

But even Santa Claus had to admit that he and his workshops did seem to be extra busy! There was so much to do! Toys to be sorted out, presents wrapped and loaded on to his sleigh . . . .

"Mind out, Prancer!" puffed Santa Claus, helping to drag a big sack of toys across the snow. "Ooh, I'll be glad to get this lot on the sleigh. Then I think we'll have a nice cup of tea . . . ."

Poor Santa! His hands were so cold that the edge of the sack slipped from his fingers.

Teddy Bears, footballs, cars, games . . . . out they all tumbled, rolling around on the snow!

Poor Prancer! He stepped back on a big, toy engine – and down he went, too!

"Prancer!" cried Santa Claus in alarm. "Prancer, are you all right?"

"No Christmas Eve duties for you, boy!" said Santa Claus seeing his hurt leg. Prancer was very upset. And Santa knew the other reindeer could not pull a heavy sleigh without him . . . .

All was quiet that Christmas Eve. Everyone had been working hard. Now all that could be heard was the rustle of coal as it shifted on the fire and the whisper of snow against the window.

Peter was fast asleep, dreaming
of everyone singing and dancing
to his guitar, just as he had told
Santa Claus. He did not hear a
low whistle outside in the snow.
But someone else did . . . .

"Here, Marcus, old boy!" called Santa Claus, as the dog appeared. "Peter told me all about you. Would you like to help pull my sleigh?" Marcus wagged his tail without stopping.

Santa Claus put on the jangly harness, just like Peter fastened the straps when Marcus pulled the sledge. But, as soon as he stepped out with the reindeer – can you guess what happened?

The sleigh lifted up into the sky, stars twinkling all around!
"Get some speed up!" cried Santa Claus, shaking the reins with a merry, jingling sound. "Lots to do before Christmas morning!"

And so there was. Hundreds of chimney stacks, thousands of roofs, across towns and big cities, farms and villages! Santa Claus and his sleigh visited them all. Marcus had never seen such sights!

Dawn was just beginning to break as Santa Claus steered the sleigh back to Peter's home. "Thanks for your help, Marcus!" he said, giving him a pat. "We'd never have managed without you!"

Peter got up early next morning. "Do you know," he said sleepily, "I had a lovely dream last night. It was all about Marcus going with Santa Claus, helping the reindeer to pull his sleigh!"

"You were asking me if I thought Marcus could do the job," Daddy smiled. "So maybe you went to bed wondering about it. Anyway, come and see what Santa Claus has left for you."

There were sweets, toys – and a big parcel with a label tied on it. "DEAR PETER," it read, "HERE IS A SPECIAL PRESENT FOR TELLING ME ABOUT YOUR DOG, MARCUS. HE WAS A GREAT HELP TO ME AND MY REINDEER!"
Peter did not know which he

liked best – the note from Santa
Claus, or the lovely guitar!
And Marcus? He settled down for
a nap. Pulling a heavy sleigh all
night long had been hard work!

Stories I have read

Christmas on the Farm ☐

Santa's Little Helper ☐

The Christmas Fairy ☐

The Night Before Christmas ☐

Santa's Busy Day ☐